THE GREAT RECESSION has been the deepest and most prolonged economic downturn ever experienced by most Americans. From the end of 2007 through 2009, more than 8 million jobs were lost. The national unemployment rate rose to more than 10 percent for the first time in nearly 30 years. Personal incomes and industrial output plunged. For many of those who managed to remain employed, wages stagnated or even declined as bonuses shriveled along with sales and profits.

Yet government employees – at the federal, state, and local levels – were largely spared the worst effects of the recession. On average, they continued receiving pay increases, even while average private sector wages dropped. When conditions were bleakest, hiring trends in America's private and public sectors were sharply divergent. At the end of 2009, state and local government employment was still nearly 2 percent higher than it had been at the recession's start in 2007, while private

sector employment had dropped more than 7 percent.

In his January 2009 inaugural address, President Barack Obama praised "the selflessness of workers who would rather cut their hours than see a friend lose their job" as an example of what "sees us through our darkest hours." Obama, however, didn't expect or ask unionized government workers to imitate their private sector counterparts. Instead, he fought for an economic "stimulus" bill that included $145 billion in state and local aid to forestall austerity measures in the public sector. In the name of promoting economic recovery, the president has been doing his best to subsidize an already wide gap in employee compensation between public and private workers.

As of March 2010, the average hourly wage in the state and local government sector was $26.25, compared with $19.58 in the private sector. Employee benefits – including health insurance, time off, and retirement – were worth an average of $13.56 per hour for state and local government employees, versus $8.15 for private employees. Combined average compensation came to $39.81 per hour for state and local government employees, versus $27.73 for private employees.

To sum it up, state and local employees enjoy a 44 percent hourly pay premium over the people they work for, according to the official data. The actual compensation gap is undoubtedly larger, because public accounting standards understate the value of retirement benefits promised to current public employees, as we'll see.

State and local employees enjoy a 44 percent hourly pay premium over the people they work for.

The federal government's roughly 3 million civilian workers had an even larger pay edge. As of 2008, the average federal employee's compensation package was worth $119,982 a year, double the estimated $59,909 compensation of private workers, according to a study by Chris Edwards of the Cato Institute. Even if the comparison is narrowed to workers with the same education and experience, the federal wage premium alone is still 24 percent, "meaning private employees must work 13½ months to earn what comparable federal workers make in 12," as researchers Andrew Biggs of the American Enterprise Institute and Jason Richwine of The Heritage Foundation have pointed out.

Like most of their state and local counterparts, federal employees also continued to receive pay raises during the recession. We

---

Like most of their state and local counterparts, federal employees also continued to receive pay raises during the recession.

---

will focus here mainly on state and local government employees, who are closest to the people who pay their salaries.

State and local government workers have for years enjoyed far more extensive and costly benefit packages than private workers. Eighty-seven percent have health insurance benefits, compared with 71 percent of private employees. Ninety percent of all state and local workers have access to an employer-sponsored retirement plan, compared with just 66 percent of private sector employees. Eighty-four percent of state and local employees have taxpayer-guaranteed pensions, while the vast majority of private workers must rely on their own retirement savings accounts. The un - funded long-term cost of generous public employee benefits – especially pensions – is a mushrooming fiscal threat across the country, as we'll also see.

To be sure, the public-private pay differential isn't uniform. It varies by occupation and by region. Across the country, though, government employees generally share an added advantage that money can't buy: much stronger job security. And the federal stimulus package was expressly designed to reinforce that security.

"Stimulating" What?

By the time private employment finally began a sluggish recovery in early 2010, state and local government employment was finally dropping. Under the circumstances, with tax revenues down and the end of supposedly temporary stimulus funding in sight, this was a predictable development. Nonetheless, it set off alarm bells in the White House. The president warned that "if additional action is not taken, hundreds of thousands of additional [government] jobs could be lost." His solution: Send another $50 billion to state and local governments. In the face of mounting public concern over federal deficit spending, even some congressional Democrats balked at rubber-stamping that request.

Raising the specter of "hundreds of thousands fewer teachers in our classrooms, fire-fighters on call and police officers on the beat," Obama's rhetoric implied that the nation's schools, firehouses, and police stations were on the verge of being staffed by skeleton crews. The numbers tell a different story. State and local government employment hit an all-time high of 19.8 million jobs in the summer of 2008, eight months after the official start of the recession. By June 2010, after falling about 240,000 jobs from that peak level, the state and local government sector still employed nearly 1.7 million more Americans than it had at the same point in 2000 – a gain of 9 percent during a decade when private employment decreased by a net 3 percent. Even as tax revenues were falling between the end of 2007 and 2009, total state and local government compensation rose by almost 6 percent – half again as fast as private sector compensation and twice the inflation rate.

The White House push for more temporary aid to states was fueled by breathless accounts of large budget gaps and cutbacks in state government employment. One of the national media's favorite sources on the subject, the Stateline.org Web site run by The Pew Center on the States, reported in the spring of 2010 that 26 states had laid off employees, 22 used furloughs to reduce pay, and 12 cut salaries outright during their 2009–10 fiscal years. Stateline's summary: "The result of all the broad-based budget cutting, now in its third consecutive year, is that state governments are shrinking."

In fact, even after those reductions, state governments employed some 22,000 more non-education workers in June 2010 than in June 2000, and nearly 200,000 more than in 1990. The state workforce "shrinkage" has been comparatively small and short-term; from a broader perspective, state payrolls are about as large as they have ever been – even excluding their burgeoning higher-education systems, which have added a quarter-million employees in the past decade. Local employment, too, jumped sharply during the decade. This increase can't be uniformly attributed to growing population or demand for services. New York State's public schools, for example, added 14,746 teachers and 8,655 non-teaching professionals to their staffs between 2000–01 and 2008–09, when their enrollment was dropping by more than 121,280 pupils.

The 2009 stimulus bill included temporary increases in federal Medicaid reimbursements to states, more federal aid to school districts enrolling high percentages of poor children, and a large "state fiscal stabilization fund" designed mainly to supplement state aid to K-12 public schools. These different aid categories were ultimately fiscal pretexts, though. Money is fungible, of course, and the ultimate effect was to put a floor under falling revenues for state governments and school districts. The main beneficiaries were public employees, whose salaries and benefits equate to more than 80 percent of state and local tax receipts.

Despite the president's rhetoric, federal stimulus aid to states wasn't contingent on saving government jobs – most of which are being "lost" through natural attrition and nonreplacement of employees, rather than outright layoffs. The stimulus also has served the unspoken purpose of financing continued wage increases for many public sector workers who, as we have seen, already earn higher average compensation than the taxpayers who are footing the bill.

Within six months of the stimulus bill's passage, tens of billions of dollars in temporary federal aid began flowing to states and school districts throughout the country, regardless of whether they had shown or planned any wage restraint. Most didn't. Total state and local wages rose by $15 billion in 2009 alone, despite the recession, according to the Bureau of Labor Statistics' Quarterly Census of Employment and Wages. While the average private sector wage was dropping along with employment on a national basis in 2009, the average annual wage for state government employees was up in 45 states, including fiscal basket cases such as Illinois, Michigan, New York, and New Jersey, according to the Bureau of Labor Statistics. The average local government wage rose at least slightly in *every* state, even crisis-wracked California. The stimulus helped make all of this possible.

This result ran counter to the advice of the pro-stimulus economists at the International Monetary Fund (IMF), among others. "Public sector wage increases should be avoided as they are not well targeted, difficult to reverse, and similar to [income] transfers in their effectiveness," the IMF staff wrote in a December 2008 report.

In fact, experience from past recessions suggests that federal spending to subsidize state and local employment won't do much to promote economic recovery, even if the money is directly targeted at creating new jobs. Consider, for example, the Comprehensive Employment and Training Act (CETA) program, which was dramatically expanded by President Jimmy Carter to help remedy sluggish job growth in the 1970s. At the program's peak in the late 1970s, state and local governments used CETA funds to create 725,000 temporary jobs – largely of the make-work variety, since unionized public employees wouldn't tolerate any competition in their own bailiwicks. This was enough all by itself to cut the unemployment rate a full percentage point in 1978. But economic conditions worsened all the same, ultimately costing Carter *his* job.

President Ronald Reagan took the opposite approach after his election in 1980, emphasizing supply-side tax cuts over demand-side government spending as the remedy for a severe double-dip recession. During the first two years of the Reagan presidency, state and local governments shed 327,000 jobs. The 1981–83 job decline in the public sector was the steepest on record, in both absolute and percentage terms; except for that period, average annual employment in state and local government increased every year from 1955 until 2009, even in recessions.

Reagan, in contrast to Obama, was unfazed by the decline in public sector employment.

He gutted CETA and reduced federal support for state and local government by eliminating dozens of aid programs. What followed, starting in 1983, was a roaring economic recovery. The Reagan boom marked a turnaround in public and private employment trends. Spurred by Great Society welfare programs, government had grown at nearly twice the rate of the private sector between 1960 and 1980. But in the next two decades, the private sector enjoyed a resurgence, creating jobs nearly twice as fast as the public sector. Since the turn of the century, the tables have turned again. From 2000 to 2007, private sector employment grew by just 3.5 percent, while the government added 7.6 percent. During the Great Recession, as noted, the disparity between the two sectors grew wider.

WAGGING THE DOG

Unions played a crucial role in the spread of America's public sector labor plague in the past half-century. While union membership has dwindled to just 7 percent of the nation's private sector workers, 37.4 percent of all public sector workers belonged to unions as of 2009. The percent of government workers covered by collective bargaining deals is highest in the local government sector, including two-thirds of teachers and solid majorities of police officers and firefighters.

Government employees now make up more than half of all union members, up from just 21 percent in 1975. Old-line industrial unions like the United Steelworkers and the United Auto Workers are shells of their former selves, while construction trade unions rely heavily on government contracting preferences and "prevailing wage" laws to keep their members

---

Unions played a crucial role in the spread of America's public sector labor plague in the past half-century.

---

working. What's left of America's organized labor movement is increasingly dominated by public employees, mainly at the state and local levels.

This is reflected by the power and prominence of government union leaders in national politics. Gerald W. McEntee, who heads the 1.6 million-member American Federation of State, County and Municipal Employees (AFSCME), has been described in *Business-Week* as the national AFL-CIO's "kingmaker" and chief political strategist. The most frequent White House visitor during Obama's first nine months in office was Andy Stern, the then-leader of the Service Employees International Union. The union represents many state and local government employees in addition to its growing presence in the increasingly federally subsidized health care sector.

While the United States as a whole has not gone the way of Canada, where 71 percent of government workers are unionized, or Great Britain, where the public sector unionization rate is 57 percent, some regions of the country have equaled or even exceeded those levels of union dominance. In New York, the most unionized state, more than 72 percent of public employees are union members. In fiscally teetering New Jersey, two-thirds of public sector workers are unionized. Union contracts cover a majority of government employees in 13 other states. Twenty-six states had laws allowing collective bargaining by virtually all public employees; 12 had laws allowing bargaining by some employee groups (such as teachers and firefighters); and 12 states made no legal provision for public-sector collective bargaining as of 2002, according to the Government Accountability Office.

The map of states with the most heavily unionized public workforces generally overlaps those without right-to-work laws. As a result, most states with union-dominated public sectors also allow "agency shop" fees – meaning that nonmembers can be forced to pay dues even if they don't want to belong to the union. This is a lucrative deal; the two national teachers unions alone collect about $2 billion in annual dues.

The financial and organizational might of unions translates into enormous political clout. As a New York City municipal labor leader exulted a generation ago, "We elect our own bosses." Across the country, those "bosses" – governors, mayors, county executives, school boards, and legislators in both parties – have responded to union political support with pay and benefit increases whose costs have strained budgets to the breaking point.

It's no coincidence that the states suffering the biggest, most intractable budget problems in the recession – California, New Jersey, New York, and the president's home state of Illinois – also are the most dominated by public sector unions. Urban historian Fred Siegel compares such unions to "the new Tammany Hall" – a force "so powerful as to threaten the Madisonian system set up to constrain any one faction from overwhelming the public interest."

Historically, public sector workers got a bit of a late start on the way to their current over-weening status on the political scene. Government workers were excluded from coverage by the landmark National Labor Relations Act of 1935, also known as the Wagner Act, which established collective bargaining rights and privileges for unions in the private sector. President Franklin D. Roosevelt, who signed the law, did not think government employees should be unionized. "The process of collective bargaining, as usually understood, cannot be transplanted into the public service," he said.

Nonetheless, beginning in the 1950s, unions spread rapidly in the public sector, as states with the most heavily unionized private sectors began passing laws authorizing collective bargaining for government employees as well. The movement got a big push in 1962, when President John F. Kennedy issued an executive order granting collective bargaining rights to federal civilian employees. By the early 1970s, public sector unions had already achieved roughly the coverage level they enjoy today.

Once government unions had gotten a foothold in roughly half the states and localities, their legislative Holy Grail became the passage of a federal Little Wagner Act, which would override any conflicting state laws and impose collective bargaining rights for public employees throughout the country. The unions came close to achieving this in the mid-1970s, when their allies in Washington included more than a few Republicans, as well as traditionally pro-union Democrats in Congress.

If they had succeeded, the fiscal condition of all 50 states might now be analogous to that of General Motors: a bankrupt ward of the federal government, dragged down by the legacy costs of a powerful labor cartel. Edwards of the Cato Institute found that while state and local government employees earn "substantially more, on average, than private sector workers in all regions of the country," those in states granting collective bargaining rights enjoy an overall compensation advantage of 42 percent over non-unionized public sector workers. Adjusting for regional labor market cost variations, "public-sector unions increase average pay levels by roughly 10 percent," Edwards estimated.

The difference between governments with unionized and non-unionized public sectors was recently highlighted in a *Washington Post*

By June 2010, the state and local government sector still employed nearly 1.7 million more Americans than it had at the same point in 2000 — a gain of 9 percent.

---

editorial contrasting the condition of "demographic cousins" Fairfax County, Va., and Montgomery County, Md., the two largest suburbs of the nation's capital. "Virginia law denies public employees collective bargaining rights; that's helped Fairfax resist budget-busting wage and benefit demands," the *Post* noted. "As revenue dipped two years ago, Fairfax officials froze all salaries for county government and school employees with little ado. By contrast, Montgomery leaders were badly equipped to cope with recession." The entire regional economy benefits from rising federal spending, but Montgomery County faces "annual deficits in the hundreds of millions of dollars as far as the eye can see," while the future is bright for Fairfax, the *Post* observed.

"Our sledgehammer, the collective bargaining process," as a former leader of the National Education Association (NEA) once described it, also has another important, if less easily quantifiable, impact in unionized states. Public employee union contracts often include myriad work rules that hinder productivity and further increase the cost of public services. Moreover, unionized public employees in some states are allowed to strike. They even have flouted laws that prohibit strikes – as in New York, where a walkout by

34,000 bus and subway workers crippled transportation in the nation's largest city for three days at the height of the Christmas shopping season in 2005.

Fortunately, the seemingly strong prospects for passage of a federal forced-unionization law covering the nation's entire public sector dissolved after a wave of strikes and labor agitation by government unions in the pivotal year of 1975. These included a mass walkout of sanitation workers and police protesting planned layoffs in a flat-broke New York City, and a strike by 75,000 Pennsylvania government employees demanding a 10 percent pay hike. ("Let's go out and close down this God-damned state," declared the Pennsylvania union leader at the time – the current nationwide AFSCME president, Gerald W. McEntee.)

As memories of that kind of labor extremism faded, the push for public sector collective bargaining made a comeback in some states. When Democrats captured the governor's offi-ces of Indiana, Missouri, and Kentucky in the late 1990s, they issued executive orders that gave collective bargaining rights to state employees. However, the orders were reversed when those offices were recaptured by Republicans.

In recent years, states permitting collective bargaining by government unions have helped those unions exploit a completely new business development strategy. Fourteen states have enabled government unions to organize nearly a quarter-million government-subsidized, home-based day care providers. The "employees" in question (60,000 in New York alone) are actually independent contractors, including friends and relatives of the working mothers whose kids they are paid to watch. Nonetheless, thanks to "agency shop" laws, they also are a new source of dues revenue and political power for the unions. Nine states also have enabled public unions to organize home care providers.

More ominously, public sector unions also continue to seek a federal end-run of state restrictions on collective bargaining. And with Obama as president, they may be a step closer to the kind of congressional victory that eluded them 35 years ago. Their trailblazing vehicle could be the Public Safety Employer-Employee Cooperation Act, which would require all states to grant union organization and collective bargaining rights to police, firefighters, and other public safety workers.

The proposed law, which has bipartisan support, would mainly affect the dozen or so states that either prohibit public sector collective bargaining or do not require it on a statewide basis. However, while most of the nation's public safety employees already have the right to bargain, the act would represent a significant foot in the door for other groups of employees. After all, they might ask if the law is enacted, is it fair for Congress to mandate collective bargaining for only *some* state and local government workers?

The nationwide unionization law for public safety employees passed in the House of Representatives in July 2010 as part of a supplemental appropriation bill for the Iraq and Afghanistan wars. Under similar circumstances in 2008, the threat of a veto by President George W. Bush was enough to derail the same bill in the Senate. This time, however, there was no sign of presidential pushback – nor did any seem likely.

"I support collective bargaining rights for all workers," Obama wrote in an October 2008 letter to the leader of the federal government's largest union. He also pledged to "review decisions by the Bush Administration that have denied these rights to federal employees and seek to restore them."

The biggest winners in Washington's stimulus sweepstakes have been teachers unions.

The letter focused on federal employees, but Obama's policies across the board have conveyed the same message: Public sector unions now have a friend in the White House.

In terms of political clout, all public employees are not equal. The biggest winners in Washington's stimulus sweepstakes have been teachers unions, whose members were the prime beneficiaries of a two-year, $53 billion federal fund expressly designed to shield them from the recession's budgetary blowback. Stimulus advocates such as House Speaker Nancy Pelosi typically promoted this as a matter of "building America's future" and "providing high quality education to all of America's students," but the political motivation was obvious. The NEA and the American Federation of Teachers have been powerful forces in the Democratic Party for decades.

In most states, well-funded teachers unions – even those without formal collective bargaining rights – are feared and courted by politicians in both parties. The California Teachers Association, to cite just one example, has spent $200 million on political activities and lobbying in the past 10 years. That state's next-largest government union group – no slouch itself – spent only half as much.

This kind of clout is reflected in the persistent growth of the public education sector, even during the worst of the Great Recession. According to U.S. Department of Labor data, local government education agencies added 125,000 people to their payrolls during the 2007–08 and 2008–09 school years. The NEA estimated that the average public school teacher salary increased by 2.9 percent in 2008–09, when the recession was at its worst.

While polls show most Americans consistently support both higher spending on schools and higher pay for teachers, most also appear to have only a fuzzy idea what schools actually spend and what teachers actually make. For example, respondents to a 2007 nationwide survey underestimated teacher salaries in their own states by an average of 30 percent.

Education researcher Jay Greene has noted that the average teacher salary – $55,350 as of 2009–10 – seems modest at first glance. However, when compared to workers of similar skill levels in similar professions, teachers are not shortchanged. In a 2007 study for the Manhattan Institute for Policy Research, Greene found that the average public school teacher was paid 36 percent more per hour than the average non-sales white-collar worker and 11 percent more than the average professional specialty and technical worker.

Thanks to tenure, most teachers enjoy even stronger job security than other public employees, although teacher layoffs loom in districts that simply can no longer afford to maintain peak staffing, wage, and benefit levels. With Obama's support, congressional Democrats responded in 2010 by proposing another $23 billion jolt of stimulus, packaged in a bill called the Keep Our Educators Working Act. It might more accurately be entitled the Keep Our Educators' Cadillac Benefits Act.

In Milwaukee, for example, the mere prospect of more federal stimulus was enough to stymie efforts by district officials to avoid 428 layoffs by having teachers share the eye-popping $26,844-per-family cost of their health insurance plans, to which the teachers currently contribute nothing at all. The teachers union wouldn't negotiate the issue. Instead, as Stephen Moore wrote in *The Wall Street Journal*:

> *The union's strategy in recent weeks has been to stage rallies demanding a federal bailout, and it used hundreds of school kids at those rallies as political props. Milwaukee's experience suggests that the $23 billion bailout fund is meant to provide a federal life raft to keep afloat the unsustainable, gold-plated compensation packages that unions negotiated when states and cities were flush with cash.*

If any state is testimony to the power of teachers unions, it is New Jersey. The Garden State spends $16,491 per pupil on K-12 education as of 2007–08, 61 percent above the national average and second only to New York, largely because its teachers are among the highest paid in the nation. Yet New Jersey has also provided an example of how politicians can stand up to teachers unions.

What's left of America's organized labor movement is increasingly dominated by public employees.

Upon taking office in January 2010, New Jersey Gov. Chris Christie inherited one of the nation's worst fiscal messes: an unprecedented $11 billion budget gap and a severely underfunded pension system. Complicating matters, the teachers union has long had its way in Trenton. Christie nonetheless began to push back, calling on teachers to begin contributing at least a tiny percentage of their salaries to health insurance premiums, proposing a tighter property tax cap opposed by the union, and urging voters to reject budgets in school districts where unions refused to accept a pay freeze. More than half of the school budgets subsequently were defeated.

"The overwhelming majority of teachers

are really good people, who care deeply about their kids and want to do a good job, but the teachers union is about the accumulation and exercise of raw power," Christie says. "The fight is about who is going to run public education in New Jersey – the parents and the people they elect, or the mindless, faceless union leaders who decide that they're going to be the ones who are going to run it because they have the money and the authority to bully school boards and local councils."

The kind of fight Christie is waging will need to be replicated in states, counties, and municipalities across the country. Federal policies, including those enacted under the guise of "economic recovery" measures, could be pivotal in determining whether parents' and taxpayers' hands are tied before those battles can even begin.

The Public Pension Bomb

Generous pensions were considered compensation for the relatively low wages paid to civil servants during the first few decades of the 20th century. By the 1970s, public sector wages began to surpass private sector norms. Nonetheless, government workers not only kept their lavish retirement benefits; they often added to them.

The standard pension model throughout most of the public sector is the defined benefit (DB) plan, which promises a stream of monthly retirement income based on an employee's longevity and end-of-career earnings. Virtually all full-time state and local employees have access to employer-sponsored retirement benefits, and 90 percent are in DB plans. Federal employees hired since 1983 are enrolled in a retirement plan that combines DB pensions with savings accounts offering guaranteed investment returns.

By contrast, only 66 percent of private sector workers had access to *any* employer-sponsored retirement benefits as of 2007, and only 21 percent could access a traditional DB pension. The vast majority of private employees with retirement benefits rely on defined-contribution (DC) savings plans, such as 401(k) accounts, whose returns are not guaranteed. The individual employee shoulders the risks of market downturns, like the more than 50 percent slump in stock prices between October 2008 and March 2009. In a DB pension plan, the sponsoring employer – which, in the public sector, ultimately means taxpayers – shoulders all the financial risks. When markets crash, taxpayers must fill the hole.

Public pension benefits are especially expensive – and their consequent liabilities especially huge – because they are also much more generous than private plans. In both union and nonunion states, most state and local pension systems allow general employees to retire as young as 55 after 30 years of service, with benefits equivalent to 60 percent or more of their average late-career salaries. Police officers and firefighters can retire even earlier, usually by age 50 or younger, after as little as 20 years on the job, with benefits equivalent to at least half of their peak pay, including overtime.

Defined benefit pensions are financed from the investment returns on large, government-sponsored retirement funds. Those funds, in turn, are fed by the contributions of employers and employees, but that burden is not equally shared between them. In most public systems, the employee share of the pension contribution is fixed at a few percentage points of the employee's salary, while the employer share fluctuates depending on how the investments are doing.

The "discount rate" applied to future obligations is a crucial determinant of a pension system's necessary funding levels: The lower the rate, the larger the contributions required to maintain "fully funded" status. Private plans must discount their liabilities based on a market rate – typically, a corporate or U.S. government bond rate – which is often much lower than the plans' projected returns. Public funds, however, are allowed to discount their long-term liabilities based on the targeted annual rate of return on their assets – which, for most public funds, was pegged at an optimistic 8 percent or higher as of 2009. The only way they can even hope to achieve that goal is by investing most of their money in risky assets, mainly stocks.

When asset returns soared to annual double-digit rates in the booming stock market of the late 1990s, many states radically reduced their pension fund contributions. Watching the boom unfold, public employee unions demanded a bigger piece of the pie for their members – and often got it, in the form of permanently increased pension benefit payouts and earlier retirement ages. One of the most egregious examples occurred in 1999 in California, when Gov. Gray Davis handed out pension sweeteners of 20 to 50 percent, including a plan under which highway patrol officers can retire at age 50 with 90 percent of their salaries.

Other states and localities seized on the soaring stock market as an opportunity for what was sold to taxpayers as a nifty arbitrage play. They issued bonds, typically at an interest rate of 5 percent or less, and "invested" the proceeds with other pension funds – which, after all, had that 8 percent target rate of return. The biggest such deal during the 1990s was New Jersey's issuance of $2.8 billion in pension bonds, which served the immediate purpose of closing a budget gap while promising to save taxpayers money in the long run.

California-style pension sweeteners and Jersey-style pension bonds came back to haunt their sponsors after the tech bubble burst on Wall Street in 2000. By autumn 2002, the stock market had dropped by nearly 40 percent from its 2000 highs, dragging down the nation's public pension fund values with it. The impact of the market downturn was most severe in cities and states that had used fiscal gimmickry to reduce their pension costs during the 1990s. The most egregious high-profile offender was San Diego, whose finances were nearly ruined by an agreement between management and union trustees to simultaneously increase benefits and shortchange the city pension fund. Meanwhile, New Jersey and other pension bond issuers found their "investment" in debt had dug their pension holes deeper, since the interest rate owed on the borrowing was more than the funds were earning.

Incredibly, some politicians ignored the lesson of this debacle. In 2003, Illinois Gov. Rod Blagojevich successfully pushed a $10 billion pension bond to plug a hole in his state budget. Among the lawmakers voting for the plan: then-state Sen. Barack Obama.

The V-shaped stock-market recovery and accompanying real estate boom between 2003 and 2007 led to a temporary stabilization of pension contribution rates, since funds based their rates on "smoothed" values over a multi-year period. It also temporarily made deals like the one in Illinois look good. But the 2007−08 market meltdown is bringing a new round of even more intense stress. With no help from Blagojevich's bond, the Illinois pension plan is easily the worst-funded in the nation, with a staggering unfunded liability of $78 billion.

The nation's largest public pension plans had unfunded liabilities of $576 billion before reflecting the full impact of the 2007–09 bear market, according to their own official statements. Using accounting standards that more accurately reflect financial risk and prospects for default, academic researchers Robert Novy-Marx of the University of Chicago and Joshua Rauh of Northwestern University estimated in a 2009 paper that pension promises already made to state and local workers are worth between $1.2 trillion and $3.2 trillion more than the assets set aside to pay for them.

Pensions aren't the only generous and underfunded long-term benefits promised to public employees. Most state and local government employees across the country also qualify for health insurance coverage after they retire – a plum offered by just 13 percent

---

Reagan, in contrast to Obama, was unfazed by the decline in public sector employment.

---

of private employers as of 2002. In contrast to pensions, retiree health benefits for government workers are funded on a pay-as-you-go basis out of state and local budgets. The nation's collective unfunded liabilities for retiree health care have been credibly estimated, by various analysts, at between $1 trillion and $1.5 trillion.

Combining pensions and retiree health care, state and local governments have promised at least $2 trillion – and perhaps as much as $4.7 trillion – in future benefits for which they haven't set aside enough money. By comparison, state and local debts to bondholders came to $2.5 trillion as of 2008.

Remember that estimated 44 percent pay premium for state and local government workers? It's larger if you translate those multitrillion-dollar pension and health care liabilities into hourly costs per employee.

Public sector pensions have proven to be unaffordable even for deep-pocketed government employers who have tried to keep up with their costs without resorting to egregious financial gimmicks. For a glimpse of what could be coming soon to a town or city near you, consider what has already happened in the nation's largest metropolis.

Without adding significantly to its municipal workforce, New York's tax-funded contribution to city employee pensions has risen from $1.1 billion in fiscal year 2001 to $7.6 billion in the 2011 city budget – an increase averaging more than $2,000 per city household over 10 years. The city's annual pension expenses now amount to 20 percent of tax collections, and it won't stop there. Pension contributions are expected to continue rising for years to come. For the amount of added money they're now pouring into pension funds every year, compared with a decade ago, New Yorkers could nearly double what they spend on police and fire protection – or rebuild their aging transit system without a borrowing a penny.

Like the public-private compensation gap, the size of the pension bomb varies across the country. Pension funds in some states, such as

Illinois and New Jersey, are flirting with insolvency after years of gimmicks and deliberate shortchanging of pension contributions. But virtually *all* public pension systems and retiree health benefit promises are seriously underfunded to some degree, when evaluated using the same accounting standards applied to private plans.

Simply put, many state and local governments have accumulated long-term debts they will not be able to repay without draconian cuts or tax hikes. Left untended, a problem this massive cannot be contained within state borders indefinitely. Like the feared Greek "contagion" of eurozone finances, it could ultimately affect the entire country. Washington could be forced to bail out the most heavily indebted states or risk another financial crisis.

So far, there's no talk of a federal bailout for troubled state pension funds, if only because the problem is both varied and enormous. But a little-noticed provision of Obama's health care overhaul bill has opened the door for federal subsidies of retiree health benefits, through the creation of a $5 billion Early Retiree Reinsurance Program to cover claims ranging from $15,000 to $90,000 for retired employees aged 55 to 65. Since state and local governments are the main source of retiree health care today, they will be the main beneficiaries of that fund.

The excessive costs and risks associated with retirement benefits for public employees are raising concerns that cross ideological lines. "One cannot both be a progressive and be opposed to pension reform," said David Crane, a San Francisco Democrat who has been a special adviser to California Gov. Arnold Schwarzenegger. Even pro-labor Democratic Party stalwarts are picking up the theme. As Pennsylvania Gov. Ed Rendell put it, "Why should state workers or city workers or county workers have benefits that are far better than private sector workers? We should have parity, not better."

Unfortunately, while governors like Rendell pay lip service to taxpayer concerns, they have done little or nothing to actually address the problem in their own backyards. Pennsylvania is only one of several states that have

> *Total state and local wages rose by $15 billion in 2009 alone, despite the recession.*

sought to minimize the visible impact of pension cost increases by adjusting contribution schedules, "smoothing" investment return assumptions over longer periods, and spreading higher annual contributions over a number of years. But this kind of tinkering merely pushed costs into the future.

Some vaunted state "pension reform" plans adopted by states around the country have been designed to marginally reduce benefit levels in the future – typically setting higher retirement ages and contribution rates for newly hired employees. A handful of states have moved some employees to "hybrid" plans that include elements of DB pensions and DC accounts, which are still more generous than the private sector norm. So far, however, no governor has followed the example of Michigan or Alaska by mandating a shift to a pure defined-contribution system for all state or local government employees, putting them on the same footing as private employees.

CONCLUSION

The 2009 federal stimulus package was just a drop in the bucket compared with the cost of benefits promised to America's current generation of public sector employees. Pension and retirement health care insurance coverage for state and local government workers across the country represent unfunded liabilities that could exceed *$2 trillion, and may reach $4.7 trillion.* Even in the Obama era, that's real money.

Combined with the federal government's own incredibly expanding debt, now approaching $10 trillion, the public sector compensation burden threatens to crush future generations of Americans. In the process, it also threatens to starve the very public services and infrastructure that government exists to provide.

To use a maxim favored by Obama Chief of Staff Rahm Emanuel, "a crisis is a terrible thing to waste." The state and local fiscal crises triggered by the Great Recession present an opportunity to concentrate public attention on the need for long-overdue structural reforms of employee compensation costs.

The day of reckoning for unsustainable state and local compensation practices cannot be put off indefinitely. However, Obama's legislative agenda – and that of congressional Democratic leaders – reflects the priorities of public sector employee unions that are the main obstacle to reform. The president's continuing push for aid to prop up the status quo is a wasted opportunity for Washington to help in promoting real change.

First American edition published in 2010 by Encounter Books,
an activity of Encounter for Culture and Education, Inc.,
a nonprofit, tax exempt corporation.
Encounter Books website address: www.encounterbooks.com

Manufactured in the United States and printed on
acid-free paper. The paper used in this publication meets
the minimum requirements of ANSI/NISO Z39.48–1992
(R 1997) (*Permanence of Paper*).

FIRST AMERICAN EDITION

LIBRARY OF CONGRESS CATALOGING-IN-PUBLICATION DATA

McMahon, E.J. (Edmund J.), 1954–
Obama and America's public sector plague / by E. J. McMahon.
p.   cm. — (Encounter broadsides)
ISBN-13: 978-1-59403-537-1 (pbk. : alk. paper)
ISBN-10: 1-59403-537-7 (pbk. : alk. paper)
1. Local officials and employees—Salaries, etc.—United States.
2. Local officials and employees—Pensions—United States.
3. United States—Officials and employees—Salaries, etc.
4. United States—Officials and employees—Pensions. I. Title.
JS361.M36   2010
331.2'81352130973—dc22
2010030407

10 9 8 7 6 5 4 3 2 1